HIROSHI SAWADA'S

THE
BARISTA
BOOK

A Coffee Lover's Companion
with Brewing Tips and Over 50 Recipes

Skyhorse Publishing

BASIC BARISTA BOOK

INTRODUCTION

Recently, professional espresso machines have been evolving, and home espresso machines have become increasingly sophisticated, making it possible to enjoy great espresso even in the comfort of home.

More and more people are training to become professional baristas, and there are a number of people who either want to open a café or who want to reproduce the taste created by a barista at home.

To free pour a design in a latte, you begin with a barista's knowledge and technique, but that's not enough to create true latte "art." Taste is also very important.

This book offers an introduction to the basic knowledge that any barista needs, along with drink recipes for espresso-based drinks that can be made at home or in a professional setting. All of the drinks featured can be made using an espresso machine. The selection is based on requests from the baristas I have trained, both in Japan and around the world, and shows how to create an actual drink menu. I have also taken into account the needs of baristas working in cafés, as all of the recipes can be made in about three minutes.

I hope this book will be useful for anyone making espresso, whether at home or in a café, bar, or restaurant.

THE BARISTA BOOK

CONTENTS

CHAPTER **6**

BARISTA RECIPES

CHAPTER 1

COFFEE BEANS

DIFFERENCES IN THE TASTE OF COFFEE BEANS

The taste of coffee beans differs depending on its origin, its blending method, and the degree of roasting.

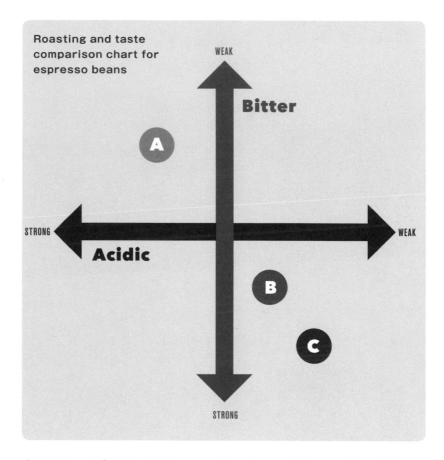

Roasting and taste comparison chart for espresso beans

WEAK

Bitter

A

STRONG — WEAK

Acidic

B

C

STRONG

As you can see from the chart, espresso beans become bitterer and less acidic when roasted dark.

common with single origin roaster
Light roast

▶ **Good match: Espresso (no sugar added), Americano**

- More acidic, less bitter. Has sweetness like a fruit.
- When milk is added, it overpowers coffee taste.
- Acidity does not pair well with milk.

Northern Italy, independent café
Medium roast

▶ **Good match: Espresso, Cappuccino**

- Slight essential oil on each bean surface can be seen.
- A good balance of bitter and rich taste with hint of chocolate.
- Tastes like bitter chocolate when you add sugar to the espresso.
- Tastes like milk chocolate when milk is added.

Southern Italy, Seattle style coffee chain
Dark roast

▶ **Good match: Latte with lots of milk, drink with flavored syrup.**

- The beans are black and shiny from essential oil.
- Tastes very bitter. Adding sugar is recommended.

# BEAN MASS
(1oz per espresso)

The taste of coffee beans differ depending on ther origin, quality, and the blending method used.

1 shot of espresso:
uses 21g beans to extract 28 mL

Adjust coffee bean mass depending on how you want to enjoy the drink. For example, to make a rich latte, use 21g of coffee beans and extract only 28 mL of espresso. To make a light latte, use less coffee and extract less espresso. The taste will differ depending on the mass of coffee beans even if you are using only one type of bean. Adjust coffee bean mass according to the type of bean, roast, and fineness of the grind.

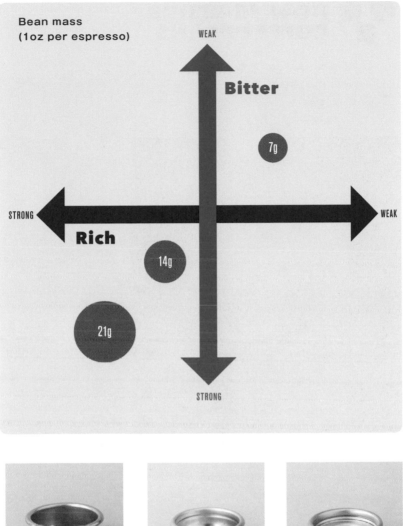

Bean mass
(1oz per espresso)

WEAK

Bitter

7g

STRONG ← → WEAK

Rich

14g

21g

STRONG

 Triple basket

 Double basket

7g Single basket

HOW TO STORE COFFEE BEANS

Important factors for bean storage conditions are temperature, humidity, oxygen, and direct sunlight. They must be all kept very low.

1 AIR-TIGHT CLOSURE

Like charcoal, beans easily absorb other smells. Avoid storing near strong smelling substances.

2 TEMPERATURE, DIRECT SUNLIGHT

Store in a cool, dark place or in a fridge.

3 HUMIDITY

Beans are subject to moisture when placed in an airtight container right after removing from a fridge. Wait until cold beans are back to room temporature to store in a container.

4 OXYGEN

Ground beans are susceptible to the air. When they come in contact with oxygen, thoy become acidic very quickly. Make sure to grind per drink.

CHAPTER 2

MACHINES & TOOLS

HOME ESPRESSO MACHINE

When selecting a home espresso machine, its function, cleaning maintenance, and design become important. Home espresso machine nowadays have high performance. They come in various colors and in stylish designs so they can be chosen based on your decorative preference.

Nespresso Lattisima +

- Insert Nespresso coffee capsule, water, and milk and then press the button to enjoy professional espresso and foamed milk
- Your cappuccino is prepared instantly
- A compact coffee maker that is both efficient and easy to clean

De'Longhi Icona Collection Espresso and Cappuccino Maker

- Machine capable of both ground coffee and cafépod
- Able to brew a variety of coffee beans
- Cupwarmer on top of the machine
- Steam nozzle lets it make fine, silky milk foam
- You can enjoy quality espresso and cappuccino using this one machine

De'Longhi Coffee Grinder

- Slow speed, precision-controlled conical grinder
- It protects coffee aroma from overheating and makes consistent particle size
- Also allows controlling fineness for desired ground coffee setting

COMMERCIAL ESPRESSO MACHINE

THE ESPRESSO MACHINE

TAMPER

Match the diameter of the piston with the type of espresso machine being used.

GRINDER

PITCHER

It is best to use a pitcher with a narrow spout to draw a thin line. Use the right size pitcher for the size of your coffee cup.

If using a bigger cup

If using a cup for macchiato or smaller cup

CHAPTER 3

ESPRESSO
PREPARATION

GRIND SETTING

To change the extraction conditions, change or adjust the grind settings. Always maintain identical dosage and keep tamping pressure consistent.

 HIGH HUMIDITY

The coffee contains moisture so the grounds are more packed and dense. Water resistance becomes high and the extraction flow rate slows down. This results in under-extraction and the espresso will taste bitter and astringent.

Solution: Adjust to a coarser grind.

 **LOW HUMIDITY**

The coffee contains less moisture and the grounds are less packed. Water flow increases and the extraction flow rate becomes faster. This results in lighter colored espresso and insufficient flavor development.

Solution: Adjust to a finer grind.

Keep espresso hopper at least ⅔ full to avoid inconsistent grinding.

DOSING AND DISTRIBUTING COFFEE

Weigh the coffee after grinding. It is important to dose the same amount consistently and to distribute evenly.

✗ BAD

Moisture on the bottom the basket will allow hot water to flow into areas that are less wet.

WHAT IS THE IDEAL WAY OF EXTRACTION?

Espresso is extracted when boiling water runs through finely ground coffee. Water tends to flow into spaces where it is less densely packed. In order to extract a good shot and to make beautiful latte art, the ground coffee must be tamped firmly and evenly.

O GOOD SHOT

Ground coffee that is evenly dosed, distributed, and tamped will allow hot water to penetrate evenly and result in a perfect espresso shot.

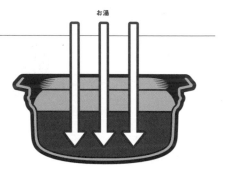

✕ BAD SHOT

Ground coffee that is unevenly dosed, distributed, and tamped will create uneven water flow through a dense area. This results in darker-colored espresso and underdeveloped flavor, which is caused by "under-extraction."

On the other hand, when hot water penetrates through a weak spot, it creates excessive water flow. This results in lighter colored espresso, an increase in bitterness, and more caffeine, which is caused by "over-extraction."

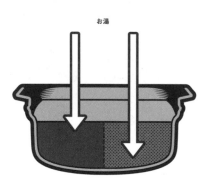

🔨 TAMPING

Tamp coffee grounds that have been dosed and distributed evenly. The key is to level the tamp and apply the same amount of force every time.

GRIPPING THE TAMPER PROPERLY

Keep your wrist straight. The espresso tamper should be a straight extension of your arm.

⭘ GOOD

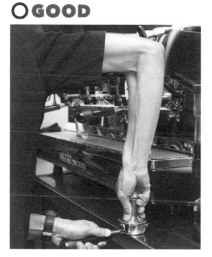

Keep your arm at 90 degrees from the porta-filter should be positioned at a perpendicular angle from your elbow down.

✕ BAD

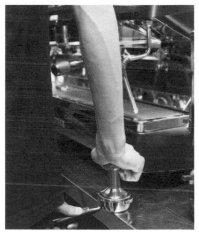

If your wrist is bent, it will cause an uneven tamp.

PROCESS

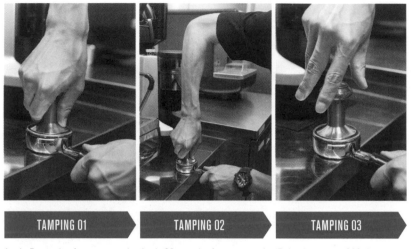

TAMPING 01	TAMPING 02	TAMPING 03
Apply 5 pounds of pressure and tamp evenly.	Apply 30 pounds of pressure and tamp evenly.	Twist the tamper 360 degrees a and polish the surface.

PROBLEM OF TAMPING

Coffee grounds that are evenly distributed in the porta-filter must have a smooth and level tamp to get a perfect shot.

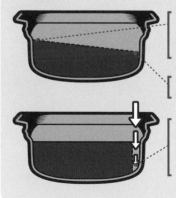

Uneven tamping results in restricted water flow at the high point and will cause insufficient extraction.

Heavy water flow at the bottom will cause over-extraction.

Tapping or hard tamping will create a gap between the coffee bed and the basket, allowing hot water to escape. This will cause insufficient extraction.

 # THE PERFECT SHOT

Begin the extraction by latching the porta-filter onto the espresso machine.

Latch the porta-filter onto espresso machine and begin the extraction. The espresso color will change from dark brown to reddish brown and to lighter brown at final phase. A good shot consists of rich and heavy crema.

The crema layer become thick, and the reddish-brown color becomes the background for latte art.

Crema is a good indicator of how well espresso has been extracted.

⭘ PERFECT ESPRESSO

- Reddish-brown color and a syrupy texture
- Thick crema that will not break easily when milk is poured
- Fresh coffee aroma
- Rich in flavor and less bitter in taste

✕ ESPRESSO HAS PALE COLOR

- Crema layer is thin and breaks easily when milked are poured
- Watery texture
- Less flavor and acidic in taste

✕ ESPRESSO HAS BLACKISH COLOR

- Coffee fat and its water content separates (there is a hole in a crema), crema does not stay intact when milk is poured
- Dark blackish color
- Astringent and bitter in taste

CHAPTER 4

PERFECTLY
TEXTURED MILK

PERFECTLY TEXTURED MILK

Maximum Fill Point

Minimum Fill Point

 STEP 1

Materials
–Milk pitcher
–Cold milk

Pour cold milk in a pitcher (do not reuse already steamed milk). It is recommended to steam with a cold pitcher and cold milk that are the same temperature.

 **STEP 2** **STRETCH**

Insert the tip of a steam wand just below the surface of the milk. Keep it stable and stretch the milk. Aim for tight, small bubbles until the temperature reaches 100° F. At 100° F, the milk should increase in volume by 1.1–1.3 times. Try to keep the stretching time short.

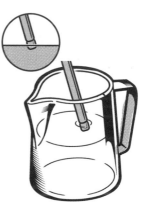

STEP 3 **ROLL**

After the temperature reaches 100° F, sink (submerse) the tip of the steam wand into the milk. Find a spot where the milk rolls, keep it stable, and burst any big bubbles. Frothed milk is light and it stays at the top, so it is not necessary to sink the steam wand too deep. At this point, do not aerate the milk.

STEP 4

Stop steaming when the temperature reaches 135–150° F, otherwise, the milk will loose its sweetness.

○ GOOD FOAM

- Has a good mouth-feel and enhances the flavor of the espresso
- Tight microfoam bubbles and a silky texture

✕ BAD FOAM

- Big coarse bubbles with no shine

TIPS

 1 Steaming pressure should always be at maximum (if the pressure is low, the bubbles will not burst).

2 Keep spinning the milk by stretching and rolling.

3 The initial bubbles that are created stay on the surface of the milk so there is no need to place steam nozzle in too deep. At this moment, foamed and steamed milk is formed inside a milk pitcher.

4 Longer rolling time results in silkier milk foam.

CHAPTER 5

FREE POUR LATTE ART

 **MECHANICS OF THE POUR**

GRIPPING THE PITCHER PROPERLY

Standard grip   Alternative grip (hold like you would a pen)

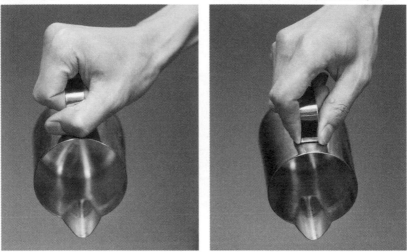

Use only your wrist and fingers to swing the pitcher. Keep your arm above the wrist stable.

SWINGING THE PITCHER

Swing the pitcher from side to side.

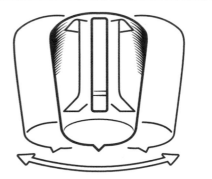

STEP 1 ▸ SINK THE MILK

Carefully and steadily pour a thin line of milk into the espresso and keep the color of crema in the background.

STEP 2 ▸ FLOAT THE MILK

Lower the tip of the pitcher close to the crema and a "white dot" will appear. At this point, the crema and foamed milk have the same density.

STEP 3 ▸ DRAW THE DESIGN

Once the "white dot" appears, gently swing the pitcher from side to side.

 CONTROLLING THE PITCHER

 **PROCESS 1** **TO SINK THE MILK**

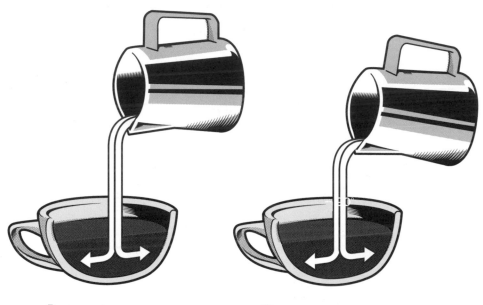

A Pour from a high point.

Raising the pitcher too high will cause the milk to dive under the crema.

B Pour at a perpendicular angle.

Pour high density milk slowly at a perpendicular angle.

Use method A or B for both Step 1 and Step 2.

PROCESS 2 **TO FLOAT THE MILK**

A Pour from a low point

Milk will float when the tip of the pitcher is close to the surface of the crema and sink if it is too far or high up.

B Pour at a low angle

Pour low density milk faster at a lower angle.

 TO DRAW A ROSETTA

STEP 1 ▶ SINK THE MILK

Carefully and steadily pour a thin line of milk into the espresso and keep the color of the crema in the background.

STEP 2 ▶ FLOAT THE MILK

You can make a Rosetta when a "white dot" appear on the surface. The density of the crema and milk foam should be equal.

STEP 3 ▶ DRAW THE DESIGN

Swing the pitcher in the center and leaves of the penumbra begin to form. Let the milk push the design forward toward the front of the cup.

STEP 4

Gradually swing the pitcher backwards to the far end of the cup.

STEP 5

Lift the pitcher off the side of the cup and pour a thin milk stream in the center, moving the pitcher forward toward your thumb.

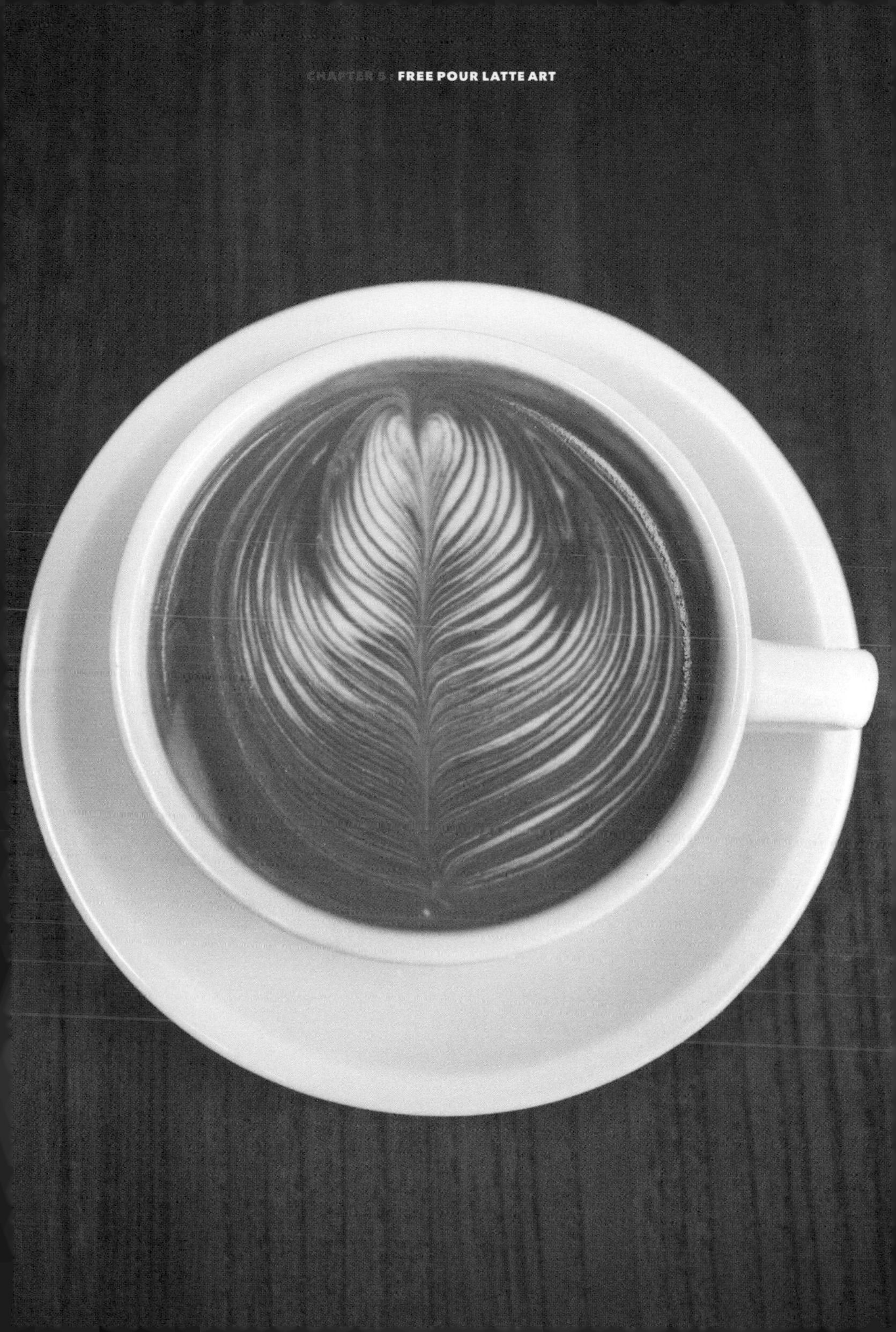

ROSETTA DRAWING TECHNIQUE

Drawing with the milk quickly can create a thin line. Drawing at a slower speed can create a thick line.

Drawing at a fast speed.

Drawing at a slower speed.

ROSETTA DRAWING TECHNIQUE

Finishing the design will be different when you change the timing of moving the pitcher backward on Step 3.

Strong Convection

Increase the milk flow and take more time to swing the pitcher at the center when the "white dot" appears. Slowly move the pitcher backwards. Convection flow happens throughout the cup.

Effective when making a big Rosetta.

Weak Convection

Decrease the milk flow and immediately swing the pitcher backwards when the "white dot" appears. Weaker convection flow happens in the cup.

Effective when making a thin or multiple Rosetta.

CAFÉ MENU RECIPE CHART

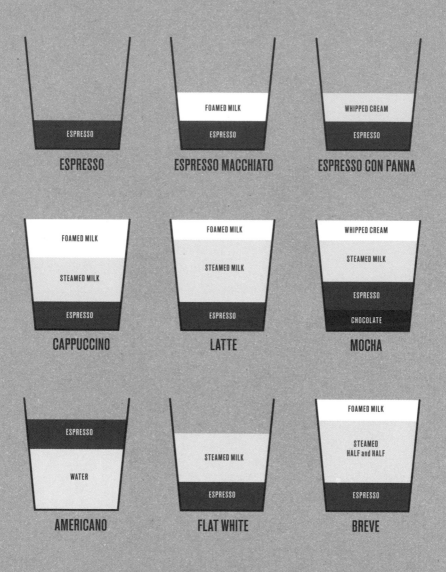

Note: *Steamed milk* is milk without foam, *foamed milk* is milk with foam.

ESPRESSO

ESPRESSO

ESPRESSO MACCHIATO

FOAMED MILK

ESPRESSO

ESPRESSO CON PANNA

WHIPPED CREAM

ESPRESSO

CAPPUCCINO

FOAMED MILK

STEAMED MILK

ESPRESSO

LATTE

FOAMED MILK

STEAMED MILK

ESPRESSO

MOCHA

WHIPPED CREAM

STEAMED MILK

ESPRESSO

CHOCOLATE

AMERICANO

ESPRESSO

WATER

FLAT WHITE

STEAMED MILK

ESPRESSO

BREVE

FOAMED MILK

STEAMED HALF and HALF

ESPRESSO

THE BARISTA BOOK

CHAPTER 6

SPECIAL ESPRESSO MACHINE
BARISTA RECIPES

ESPRESSO
Espresso-based drink

INGREDIENTS [1 SERVING]

· Espresso, 1 shot (25–30 ml)

DIRECTIONS

 STEP 1 Extract espresso into cup.

TIP

Preheat your cup and ensure it is an appropriate size. Crema loses the richness of its flavor when disturbed, so it is strongly recommended that it is drank as soon as possible after serving.

ESPRESSO MACCHIATO

Equal parts foamed milk and espresso

INGREDIENTS [1 SERVING]

- Espresso, 1 shot (25–30 ml)
- Milk, 25–30 ml

DIRECTIONS

STEP 1 Extract espresso into cup.

STEP 2 Steam milk in a pitcher equal in size to that of the cup of espresso.

STEP 3 Pour silky foamed milk over espresso.

TIP

Silky foamed milk (free of bubbles) has a better and more satisfying taste.

BASIC COFFEE

AMERICANO
Espresso and hot water

INGREDIENTS [1 SERVING]

- Espresso, 1 shot (25–30 ml)
- Hot water, 200 ml

DIRECTIONS

 Pour hot water into cup.

 Extract espresso over hot water.

TIP

Just like diluting shochu, adding the extracted espresso to the hot water conserves the flavor's richness.

BASIC COFFEE

ICE AMERICANO
Ice water with espresso

INGREDIENTS [1 SERVING]

- Espresso, 1 shot (25–30 ml)
- Water, 100 ml
- Ice (a suitable amount)

DIRECTIONS

 STEP 1   Put water and ice in cup.

 STEP 2   Extract espresso into cup, melting the ice into water.

TIP

There will be a beautiful lighter color to the drink due to the sudden cooling of the espresso. Add milk or gum syrup to your liking up to within ¼ inch of the lip of the cup.

CAFFÉ LATTE

Espresso with a good quantity of milk

INGREDIENTS [1 SERVING]

- Espresso, 1 shot (25–30 ml)
- Milk, 300 ml

DIRECTIONS

 STEP 1 Extract espresso into cup.

 STEP 2 Steam milk in a pitcher equal in size to that of the cup of espresso.

 STEP 3 Pour foamed milk and steamed milk into cup. Leaving ¼ inch of foamed milk on the top is recommended.

TIP

Formed Milk

Steamed Milk

It is extremely important to have silky foamed milk in order to be able to create latte art.

Add the foamed and steamed milk to the espresso as soon as possible before they separate. For best results they should not separate until they have been added to the espresso.

BASIC COFFEE

ICE CAFFÉ LATTE

A perfect drink for a hot days

INGREDIENTS [1 SERVING]

- Espresso, 1 shot (25–30 ml)
- Milk, 200 ml
- Ice (a suitable amount)

DIRECTIONS

STEP 1 Pour chilled milk into glass.

STEP 2 Add espresso.

STEP 3 Add ice.

Too keep your café latte from becoming watery, be sure to not add the ice until last.

BASIC COFFEE

LATTE MACCHIATO

Espresso macchiato on the surface of foamed milk

INGREDIENTS [1 SERVING]

- Espresso, single ristretto shot (15–20 ml)
- Milk, 200 ml

DIRECTIONS

 STEP 1 Prepare three parts foamed milk to seven parts steamed milk. (ex. a 200 ml cup will require 60 ml of foamed milk and 140 ml of steamed milk.)

 STEP 2 Pour mixture into cup.

 STEP 3 Pour single ristretto espresso shot into the center of the milk mixture.

TIP

An important part of this single ristretto shot drink is that it has more foamed milk than a café latte. Pouring the espresso that is seen in the picture is recommended.

BREVE

A rich-tasting drink with milk and cream

INGREDIENTS [1 SERVING]

- Espresso, 1 shot (25–30 ml)
- Milk, 100 ml
- Cream, 100 ml

DIRECTIONS

STEP 1 Extract espresso into cup.

STEP 2 Add equal parts of milk and cream to pitcher and steam.

STEP 3 Combine espresso, steamed milk, and cream mixture.

TIP

You can freely adjust the amount of milk used depending upon the percentage of butterfat present in your cream.

BASIC COFFEE

CAFFÉ MOCHA

The popular combination of espresso and chocolate sauce

INGREDIENTS [1 SERVING]

- Espresso, 1 shot (25–30 ml)
- Chocolate sauce, 1 tablespoon (15 ml)
- Milk, 100 ml
- Whipped Cream, a suitable amount

DIRECTIONS

STEP 1 Pour chocolate sauce into cup.

STEP 2 Add espresso.

STEP 3 Steam milk in a pitcher equal in size to that of the cup of espresso. Add whipped cream if desired.

TIP

Use a stirrer if the chocolate sauce does not adequately melt into the espresso. Steam your milk warmer than usual if you wish to top your drink with cold whipped cream as the temperature will lower.

ICED MOCHA

A drink thickened with chocolate sauce

INGREDIENTS [1 SERVING]

- Espresso, 1 shot (25–30 ml)
- Chocolate sauce, 1 tablespoon (15 ml)
- Milk, 200 ml
- Ice (a suitable amount)

DIRECTIONS

STEP 1 Put chocolate sauce into cup.

STEP 2 Add espresso. Mix with stirrer until completely blended.

STEP 3 Pour milk. Add ice.

TIP

Chocolate will blend easier with espresso with the use of a stirrer.

BASIC COFFEE

TIP

If desired, add sugar to the top layer of foamed milk and eat with a spoon.

DRY CAPPUCCINO

Espresso with more than half a cup of foamed milk

INGREDIENTS [1 SERVING]

- Espresso, 1 shot (25–30 ml)
- Milk, 180 ml

DIRECTIONS

STEP 1 Steam milk in a pitcher equal in size to that of the cup of espresso. In order to increase the amount of foamed milk, add more air than usual.

STEP 2 Extract espresso into cup while foamed and steamed milk is being prepared, not before or after, so that sufficient separation occurs.

STEP 3 Lastly add steamed milk to espresso and spoon foamed milk onto the top.

WET CAPPUCCINO

Cappuccino prepared in a cup smaller than that used for lattes

INGREDIENTS [1 SERVING]

- Espresso, 1 shot (25–30 ml)
- Milk, 180 ml

DIRECTIONS

 STEP 1 Extract espresso into cup.

STEP 2 Prepare steamed and foamed milk in a pitcher equal in size to that of the cup of espresso.

STEP 3 Pour foamed milk and steamed milk into cup. Leaving ¼ inch of foamed milk on the top is recommended.

TIP

See page P29 for the proper method to make foamed milk.

ICED CAPPUCCINO

A cold foam drink enjoyed without a straw

INGREDIENTS [1 SERVING]

- Espresso, 1 shot (25–30 ml)
- Milk, 200 ml

DIRECTIONS

STEP 1 Pour milk into pitcher, steam milk until lukewarm.

STEP 2 Extract espresso into cup, add only lukewarm foamed milk.

STEP 3 Pour in cold milk. Lastly, add ice.

TIP

Foamed milk will rise naturally to the top. If lukewarm steamed milk is too hot, it will melt the ice.

BASIC COFFEE

CAFÉ AU LAIT

The French, coffee-milk mix of strong coffee and streamed milk

INGREDIENTS [1 SERVING]

- Espresso, 1 shot (25–30 ml)
- Hot water, 70 ml
- Milk, 200 ml

DIRECTIONS

STEP 1   Pour hot water into cup.

STEP 2   Extract espresso.

STEP 3   Steam milk in a pitcher equal in size to that of the cup of espresso. Then, pour into cup.

TIP

The steamed milk is the most important part of a delicious café au lait.

BASIC COFFEE

FLAT WHITE

The popular New Zealand / Australian espresso drink with less foamed milk than a café latte or a cappuccino

INGREDIENTS [1 SERVING]

- Espresso, 1 shot (25–30 ml)
- Milk, 180 ml

DIRECTIONS

 STEP 1 Extract espresso.

 STEP 2 Prepare steamed and foamed milk in a pitcher equal in size to that of the cup of espresso and pour into cup.

STEP 3 Pour foamed milk and steamed milk into cup.

STRAWBERRY MACCHIATO

JANUARY: The best way to enjoy strawberry season

INGREDIENTS [1 SERVING]

- Espresso, single ristretto shot (15–20 ml)
- Strawberry syrup, 1 tablespoon (15 ml)
- Milk, 200 ml

DIRECTIONS

STEP 1 Pour strawberry syrup into cup.

STEP 2 Prepare three parts foamed milk to seven parts steamed milk. (ex., a 200 ml cup will require 60 ml of foamed milk and 140 ml of steamed milk.) Pour steamed milk first, and then foamed milk.

STEP 3 Pour single ristretto espresso shot into the center of the milk mixture.

MINT MOCHA

FEBRUARY: How about a little kick of mint flavor on Valentine's Day?

INGREDIENTS [1 SERVING]

- Espresso, 1 shot (25–30 ml)
- Mint syrup, 1 tablespoon (15 ml)
- Chocolate sauce, 1 tablespoon (15 ml)
- Milk, 200 ml

DIRECTIONS

 STEP 1 Combine mint syrup and chocolate sauce in cup.

STEP 2 Add espresso and mix well.

STEP 3 Prepare steamed and foamed milk in a pitcher equal in size to that of the cup of espresso and pour into cup. Create latte art and add cinnamon stick if desired.

WHITE CHOCOLATE MACCHIATO

MARCH: Celebrate the end of winter with this delicious treat

INGREDIENTS [1 SERVING]

- Espresso, single ristretto shot (15–20 ml)
- Vanilla syrup, 1 tablespoon (15 ml)
- White chocolate sauce, 1 tablespoon (15 ml)
- Milk, 200 ml

DIRECTIONS

STEP 1 Pour vanilla syrup into cup.

STEP 2 Prepare three parts foamed milk to seven parts steamed milk. (ex., a 200 ml cup will require 60 ml of foamed milk and 140 ml of steamed milk.) Pour steamed milk first, and then foamed milk.

STEP 3 Pour single ristretto espresso shot into the center of the milk mixture. Then, create crisscrossing pattern out of chocolate syrup.

TIP

You can use caramel sauce instead of white chocolate to create a caramel Macchiato. The crisscross pattern recommended for the application of the white chocolate can be seen in the picture.

SEASONAL DRINKS

TIP

Add cinnamon powder if you like.

BANANA BREAD LATTE

APRIL: A drink that has the flavor of freshly baked banana bread

INGREDIENTS [1 SERVING]

- Espresso, 1 shot (25–30 ml)
- Banana syrup, 1½ teaspoons (7.5 ml)
- Gingerbread syrup, 1½ teaspoons (7.5 ml)
- Milk, 200 ml

DIRECTIONS

STEP 1 Pour banana syrup and gingerbread syrup in cup.

STEP 2 Add espresso and mix well.

STEP 3 Prepare steamed and foamed milk in a pitcher equal in size to that of the cup of espresso and pour into cup. Create latte art if desired.

BLACK CHERRY MOCHA

MAY: A sweet cherry and chocolate drink

INGREDIENTS [1 SERVING]

- Espresso, 1 shot (25–30 ml)
- Black Cherry Syrup, 1 tablespoon (15 ml)
- Chocolate sauce, 1 tablespoon (15 ml)
- Milk, 200 ml

DIRECTIONS

STEP 1 Pour black cherry syrup and chocolate sauce into cup.

STEP 2 Add espresso and mix well.

STEP 3 Prepare steamed and foamed milk in a pitcher equal in size to that of the cup of espresso and pour into cup. Create latte art if desired.

SEASONAL DRINKS

ICED SPICE MOCHA
JUNE: Spice up your break with an exotic drink

INGREDIENTS [1 SERVING]

- Espresso, 1 shot (25–30 ml)
- Spiced chai syrup, 1 tablespoon (15 ml)
- Chocolate sauce, 1 tablespoon (15 ml)
- Milk, 200 ml
- Ice (a suitable amount)

DIRECTIONS

STEP 1 Pour spiced chai syrup and chocolate sauce into glass.

STEP 2 Add espresso and mix well.

STEP 3 Pour milk. Lastly, add ice.

TIP

You can also try using ginger in place of spiced chai syrup.

SEASONAL DRINKS

ICED VALENCIA MOCHA

JULY: Refresh yourself with this citrus drink during the peak of summer

INGREDIENTS [1 SERVING]

- Espresso, 1 shot (25–30 ml)
- Chocolate sauce, 1 tablespoon (15 ml)
- Orange syrup, 1 tablespoon (15 ml)
- Milk, 200 ml
- Ice (a suitable amount)

DIRECTIONS

STEP 1 Pour chocolate sauce into glass.

STEP 2 Add espresso and mix well.

STEP 3 Put orange syrup into glass. Pour milk carefully. Lastly, add ice.

TIP

If you pour the milk carefully enough, it will create a gradation from white to orange.

SEASONAL DRINKS

ICED COCONUT LATTE

AUGUST: A drink reminiscent of the seaside in midsummer

INGREDIENTS [1 SERVING]

- Espresso, 1 shot (25–30 ml)
- Coconut flakes, a suitable amount
- Coconut syrup, 1 tablespoon (15 ml)
- Milk, 200 ml
- Ice (a suitable amount)

DIRECTIONS

STEP 1 Rim the glass in coconut flakes.

STEP 2 Put coconut syrup into glass. Add espresso.

STEP 3 Pour iced milk. Lastly, add ice.

TIP

Rimming the glass in syrup before adding the coconut flakes will result in the best snow-like effect.

SEASONAL DRINKS

TIP

Swapping out the caramel sauce for chocolate sauce is just as tasty.

MAPLE BACON LATTE

SEPTEMBER: Saltiness and sweetness that surprises you with how well they suit one another

INGREDIENTS [1 SERVING]

- Espresso, 1 shot (25–30 ml)
- Maple syrup, 1 tablespoon (15 ml)
- Milk, 200 ml
- Bacon bits, a suitable amount
- Caramel sauce, a suitable amount

DIRECTIONS

STEP 1 Pour maple syrup into cup. Add espresso and mix well.

STEP 2 Prepare steamed and foamed milk in a pitcher equal in size to that of the cup of espresso and pour into cup.

STEP 3 Sprinkle bacon bits. Add caramel sauce at the very end.

SALTED CARAMEL LATTE

OCTOBER: A drink utilizing the famous caramel of Bretagne

INGREDIENTS [1 SERVING]

- Espresso, 1 shot (25–30 ml)
- Caramel syrup, 1 tablespoon (15 ml)
- Milk, 200 ml
- Salt, a suitable amount

DIRECTIONS

STEP 1 Rim cup in salt (see page 80), pour in caramel syrup.

STEP 2 Add espresso and mix well.

STEP 3 Prepare steamed and foamed milk in a pitcher equal in size to that of the cup of espresso and pour into cup. Create latte art if desired.

TIP

Adding caramel sauce helps bring out the flavor.

SEASONAL DRINKS

TIP

Substituting Baileys
with Kahlua is equally
delicious.

BAILEYS'S MOCHA

NOVEMBER: Chocolate liquor to warm you up

INGREDIENTS [1 SERVING]

- Espresso, 1 shot (25–30 ml)
- Baileys, 1 tablespoon (15 ml)
- Chocolate sauce, 1 tablespoon (15 ml)
- Milk, 200 ml

DIRECTIONS

STEP 1 Pour Baileys and chocolate sauce into cup.

STEP 2 Add espresso and mix well.

STEP 3 Prepare steamed and foamed milk in a pitcher equal in size to that of the cup of espresso and pour into cup. Create latte art if desired.

GINGERBREAD LATTE

DECEMBER: A Christmas cookie drink to suit the season

INGREDIENTS [1 SERVING]

- Espresso, 1 shot (25–30 ml)
- Gingerbread syrup, 1 tablespoon (15 ml)
- Milk, 200 ml

DIRECTIONS

STEP 1 Pour gingerbread syrup into cup.

STEP 2 Add espresso and mix well.

STEP 3 Prepare steamed and foamed milk in a pitcher equal in size to that of the cup of espresso and pour into cup. Create latte art if desired.

TIP

We also recommend the addition of ginger extract and chocolate sauce.

ICED REVOLVER LATTE

The popular iced latte served in an original design glass jar

INGREDIENTS [1 SERVING]

- Espresso (STREAMER Blend), 50 ml (25 ml × 2)
- Milk (3.6% milk fat), 280 ml
- Ice, a suitable amount

DIRECTIONS

STEP 1 Pour iced milk into ice cold glass.

STEP 2 Extract 25 ml of espresso into two shot glasses,
each with 22 grams of ground coffee beans.

STEP 3 Combine shots into glass jar. Lastly, add ice and serve.

TIP

One shot usually requires 7 grams of coffee beans, while this indulgent drink uses about six times that amount—hence the name "revolver."

STREAMER SECRET RECIPES

SUPER STREAMER LATTE

The famously strong Streamer Coffee café latte

INGREDIENTS [1 SERVING]

- Espresso (STREAMER Blend), 50 ml (25 ml × 2)
- Milk (3.6% milk fat), 280 ml

DIRECTIONS

 STEP 1 Extract 25 ml of espresso into two shot glasses, each with 22 grams of ground coffee beans.

 STEP 2 Steam milk in pitcher to 142° F, prepare foamed and steamed milk.

 STEP 3 Create latte art while pouring.

 TIP

Milk reaches its maximum sweetness at 142° F, to the point it will not even require sugar.

THE MILITARY LATTE

The military latte—STREAMER's signature drink

INGREDIENTS [1 SERVING]

- Espresso (STREAMER Blend), 25 ml
- Matcha powder, two teaspoons
- Hot water, a minimal amount
- White chocolate sauce, one tablespoon (15 ml)
- Milk (3.6% milk fat), 280 ml
- Cocoa powder, a suitable amount

DIRECTIONS

STEP 1 Put matcha powder in cup, add just a little bit of hot water and mix.

STEP 2 Add white chocolate sauce and mix thoroughly.
Sprinkle cocoa powder over mixture.

STEP 3 Steam milk in pitcher to 142°F,
prepare foamed and steamed milk.

STEP 4 Create a leaf design while pouring.

STEP 5 Add one shot of espresso with 22 grams of ground coffee
beans and serve.

TIP

If the leaf is drawn properly, it
will form the military design.

ICED CANDY LATTE

The latte featuring Osaka's famous Hiyashi Ame

INGREDIENTS [1 SERVING]

- Espresso, 1 shot (25–30 ml)
- Hiyashi Ame, at least 3½ tablespoons (55 ml)
- Milk, 150 ml
- Ice (a suitable amount)

DIRECTIONS

STEP 1 Put Hiyashi Ame into glass and mix in milk well.

STEP 2 Add espresso.

STEP 3 Add ice, and serve.

TIP

The milk can be substituted with water. Pouring in the espresso slowly will create two separate layers inside your cup.

Osaka's famous Hiyashi Ame by Katashimo

ARRANGED DRINK

ICED MILO LATTE

A mix of Nestlé Milo chocolate and espresso

INGREDIENTS [1 SERVING]

- Espresso, 1 shot (25–30 ml)
- Nestlé Milo, 1 tablespoon
- Milk, 150 ml

DIRECTIONS

 STEP 1 Add milo into glass, mix in milk.

STEP 2 Add espresso.

CINNAMON CARAMEL LATTE

Café latte that tastes like a cinnamon roll!

INGREDIENTS [1 SERVING]

- Espresso, 1 shot (25–30 ml)
- Cinnamon syrup, 1½ teaspoons (7.5 ml)
- Caramel syrup, 1½ teaspoons (7.5 ml)
- Milk, 200 ml

DIRECTIONS

STEP 1   Add cinnamon syrup and caramel syrup into cup.

STEP 2   Add espresso, mix well.

STEP 3   Prepare steamed and foamed milk in a pitcher equal in size to that of the cup of espresso and pour into cup. Create latte art and add cinnamon stick if desired.

TIP

Adjust amounts of caramel and cinnamon to suit your own tastes. See page 36 for instructions on creating a rosetta design.

ARRANGED DRINK

ESPRESSO COLA

The bitterness of espresso fused with the sweetness of soda

INGREDIENTS [1 SERVING]

- Espresso, single ristretto shot (15-20 ml)
- Coca Cola, 1 can (190 ml)
- Ice (a suitable amount)

DIRECTIONS

 Put a suitable amount of ice into glass, and add cola very carefully.

 Add espresso and serve.

TIP

For when you want an espresso and a cola at the same time. Take care not to add too much espresso or the temperature of the drink will rise too much.

FRESH MINT AMERICANO

A refreshing iced coffee with mint leaves that you'll want to drink in warm weather

INGREDIENTS [1 SERVING]

- Espresso, 1 shot (25–30 ml)
- Mint leaves, approximately 20–30 leaves
- Gum syrup (to taste)
- Lemon juice (to taste)
- Water, 100 ml
- Ice (a suitable amount)

DIRECTIONS

STEP 1   Put mint leaves in glass and lightly crush.

STEP 2   Add gum syrup and lemon juice, then add ice water.

STEP 3   Add ice, and lastly pour espresso into mixture.

TIP

Be careful not to crush the mint leaves too thoroughly or they will make your drink bitter. We recommend crushing only to the degree seen in the picture, which is about when you will be able to begin smelling the mint aroma.

FLAT BROWN

A delicious drink with milk and espresso

INGREDIENTS [1 SERVING]

- Espresso, 1 shot (25–30 ml)
- Milk, 30 ml

DIRECTIONS

 STEP 1 Add cold milk to a small glass.

 STEP 2 Add espresso and serve.

TIP

Enjoy the flavor of espresso in your first sip. Then, the sweetness of the milk comes after when you have another sip.

ARRANGED DRINK

SPICY MAYA MOCHA

Chocolate with a spicy sensation

INGREDIENTS [1 SERVING]

- Espresso, 1 shot (25–30 ml)
- Cinnamon syrup, 1 tablespoon (15 ml)
- Chocolate sauce, 1 tablespoon (15 ml)
- Milk, 200 ml
- Red pepper or cayenne pepper, to taste

DIRECTIONS

STEP 1 Add cinnamon syrup and chocolate sauce to cup.

STEP 2 Add preferred amount of red pepper, pour in espresso and mix.

STEP 3 Prepare steamed and foamed milk in a pitcher equal in size to that of the cup of espresso and pour into cup. Then, pour into cup.

TIP

Do not add too much red pepper! We recommend no more than the amount seen in the picture.

ARRANGED DRINK

TIP

The chai syrup acts in harmony with the spiciness of the wasabi for an enjoyable drink.

TOKYO STYLE LATTE

Tokyo's famous Edo Mae Zushi-inspired spicy latte with wasabi

INGREDIENTS [1 SERVING]

- Espresso, 1 shot (25–30 ml)
- Wasabi powder, ¼ teaspoon (Adjust amount to your taste)
- Spiced chai syrup, 1 tablespoon (15 ml)
- Milk, 200 ml
- Ice (a suitable amount)

DIRECTIONS

STEP 1   Put wasabi powder and spiced chai syrup into glass.

STEP 2   Add espresso and mix well.

STEP 3   Pour milk. Lastly, add ice, and serve.

KYOTO STYLE LATTE

A drink that inspires imagery of Kyoto's famous matcha, boiled tofu, and tofu sheets

INGREDIENTS [1 SERVING]

- Espresso, 1 shot (25–30 ml)
- Matcha powder, 1 tablespoon
- Hot water, a minimal amount
- Condensed milk, 1 tablespoon (20 ml)
- Soy milk, 200 ml
- Ice (a suitable amount)

DIRECTIONS

 STEP 1 Combine matcha powder and a minimal amount of hot water in cup and mix well until completely blended.

 STEP 2 Add condensed milk and mix well.

STEP 3 Pour soy milk. Then add espresso, and lastly add ice.

TIP

Adding too much hot water will thin the milk, so be careful.

ARRANGED DRINK

ARRANGED DRINK

SHIBIRE MOCHA

Spicy drink that has a kick of Japanese pepper

INGREDIENTS [1 SERVING]

- Espresso, 1 shot (25–30 ml)
- Spiced chai syrup, 1 tablespoon (15 ml)
- Chocolate sauce, 1 tablespoon (15 ml)
- Milk, 200 ml
- Japanese pepper (a pinch)

DIRECTIONS

STEP 1 Add spiced chai syrup and chocolate sauce.

STEP 2 Add a pinch of Japanese pepper. Then, add espresso and mix.

STEP 3 Prepare steamed and foamed milk in a pitcher equal in size to that of the cup of espresso and pour into cup.

TIP

The recommended amount of chocolate sauce and chai syrup is seen in the picture. Do not add too much Japanese pepper! It may numb your tongue.

ARRANGED DRINK

VANILLA SOY LATTE

The perfect combination of vanilla and soy milk

INGREDIENTS [1 SERVING]

- Espresso, 1 shot (25–30 ml)
- Vanilla syrup, 1 tablespoon (15 ml)
- Soy milk, 30 ml

DIRECTIONS

 STEP 1 Pour vanilla syrup into cup.

 STEP 2 Add espresso.

 STEP 3 Prepare steamed and foamed milk in a pitcher equal in size to that of the cup of espresso and pour into cup. Create latte art and add cinnamon stick if desired.

 TIP Blended soybean milk is recommended!

RED EYE

Popular on the East Coast of the US

INGREDIENTS [1 SERVING]

- Espresso, 1 shot (25–30 ml)
- Drip Coffee, 200 ml

DIRECTIONS

 STEP 1 Prepare drip coffee in a cup.

 STEP 2 Add espresso.

TIP

For those New Yorkers who fly to the West Coast and back in the same day on business and need to stay awake through the night. The red eyes of those workaholics inspired the name of this drink with the extra caffeine they need to keep going.

ARRANGED DRINK

TERIYAKI LATTE

A latte that has the taste of a flan's caramel layer

INGREDIENTS [1 SERVING]

- Espresso, 1 shot (25–30 ml)
- Vanilla syrup, 1 tablespoon (15 ml)
- Soy sauce, a few drops
- Milk, 200 ml

DIRECTIONS

STEP 1 ▶ Pour vanilla syrup into a cup and add a few drops of soy sauce.

STEP 2 ▶ Add espresso.

STEP 3 ▶ Prepare steamed and foamed milk in a pitcher equal in size to that of the cup of espresso and pour into cup. Then, pour into cup.

TIP

We recommend no more than the amount of soy sauce seen in the picture. Traditionally, a small amount of soy sauce is added to sweets to enhance their flavor. Enjoy the harmony of coffee and soy sauce.

EGGNOG LATTE

A simpler than usual recipe for Eggnog, a popular drink throughout the United States and Canada during the Christmas season

INGREDIENTS [1 SERVING]

- Espresso, 1 shot (25–30 ml)
- Egg yolk, 1 (the fresher the better)
- Irish cream syrup, 1 tablespoon (15 ml)
- Spiced chai syrup, 1½ teaspoons (7.5 ml)
- Milk, 200 ml

DIRECTIONS

STEP 1 Combine yoke, Irish cream syrup, and spiced chai syrup in a glass.

STEP 2 Add espresso.

STEP 3 Prepare steamed and foamed milk in a pitcher equal in size to that of the cup of espresso and pour into cup. Then, pour into cup little by little.

TIP

Do not let your steamed milk get too hot or it will harden the egg yolk.

TIP

Adding the espresso will create froth. Enjoy espresso-flavored beer froth.

ESPRESSO BEER

A bitter drink similar to black beer

INGREDIENTS [1 SERVING]

- Espresso, single ristretto shot (15–20 ml)
- Beer, 1 can (350 ml)
- Ice (a suitable amount)

DIRECTIONS

STEP 1 Put ice in glass. Then, pour beer over ice very carefully.

STEP 2 Add espresso, and serve.

SHOCHU AMERICANO

A drink that celebrates the perfect combination of mugi shochu and coffee

INGREDIENTS [1 SERVING]

- Espresso, 1 shot (25–30 ml)
- Mugi Shochu, 150 ml
- Ice (a suitable amount)

DIRECTIONS

 STEP 1 Put ice into glass. Then, pour mugi shochu over ice.

STEP 2 Add espresso.

 TIP

Mugi Shochu suits coffee better than imo shochu.

ESPRESSO COCKTAIL

HOT APPLE CIDER

A drink reminiscent of hot apple pie, popular with children and adults alike

INGREDIENTS [1 SERVING]

- Apple Juice, 200 ml
- Spiced chai syrup (or cinnamon powder), 1½ teaspoons (7.5 ml)

DIRECTIONS

STEP 1 Pour spiced chai syrup into microwaveable glass.

STEP 2 Steam apple juice to 167° F.

STEP 3 Pour steamed apple juice into the microwaveable glass of spiced chai syrup.

TIP

We recommended using light-colored apple juice.

HOT CHOCOLATE

A classic with a hint of secret vanilla flavor

INGREDIENTS [1 SERVING]

- Chocolate sauce, 1 tablespoon (15 ml)
- Vanilla syrup, 1½ teaspoons (7.5 ml)
- Milk, 200 ml
- Cocoa powder, a suitable amount

DIRECTIONS

 STEP 1 Pour chocolate sauce and vanilla syrup into cup.

 STEP 2 Prepare steamed and foamed milk in a pitcher equal in size to that of the cup.

 STEP 3 Add a tiny amount foamed and steamed milk to chocolate sauce and vanilla syrup mixture and mix until blended. Sprinkle cocoa powder over top and then add remaining milk. Create whatever latte art is desired.

TIP

The secret is the addition of vanilla flavoring enhancing the richness of the drink.

STEAMED MENU

MILKY-CCINO

The richness of hot CALPIS with milk

INGREDIENTS [1 SERVING]

- CALPIS, 3 tablespoons (45 ml)
- Milk, 200 ml

DIRECTIONS

STEP 1 Pour CALPIS and milk into a pitcher and mix.

STEP 2 Prepare steamed and foamed milk in a pitcher.

STEP 3 Pour steamed and foamed milk into cup.

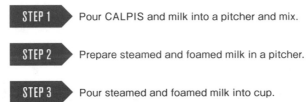

TIP

Spooning foamed milk in last will create the fluffiest, most delicious looking appearance.

CALPIS® is a registered trademark of Calpis Co., Ltd.

MISO-CCINO

Add foamed milk and fashion a cappuccino out of miso soup

INGREDIENTS [1 SERVING]

- Miso broth (self-prepared or store bought), 1 tablespoon
- Hot water, 80 ml
- Milk, 80 ml
- Dried seaweed, a suitable amount
- Flaked seaweed, a suitable amount

DIRECTIONS

STEP 1 Add miso broth to a Japanese bowl, fill half of bowl with hot water and blend.

STEP 2 Steam milk with espresso machine, prepare foamed milk and steamed milk.

STEP 3 Sprinkle flaked seaweed over broth, pour milk into mixture.

NOODLE-CCINO

Add foamed milk and fashion a drink that is both rich and mild

INGREDIENTS [1 SERVING]

- Curry flavored cup ramen (one serving)
- Hot water, 150 ml
- Milk, 150 ml

DIRECTIONS

STEP 1   Prepare cup ramen according to instructions.

STEP 2   Put in your favorite cup.

STEP 3   Prepare steamed milk and foamed milk in espresso machine only until simmering. Pour milk into cup.

COMPATIBLE FOOD

ESPRESSO

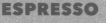

Vanilla ice cream

Affogato—Espresso poured over vanilla ice cream. Combination of cold and warm/sweet and bitter.

Chocolate truffle

Great combination of rich chocolate and strong espresso.

AMERICANO
(LIGHT ROAST)

Sandwich

Salty taste brings out the sweetness of coffee.

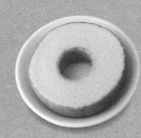

Baumkuchen

Aromatic baumkuchen pairs well with refreshing coffee. They compliment each other well.

WITH ESPRESSO

AMERICANO
(DARK ROAST)

LATTE

Cheesecake

Rich and heavy cream cheese pairs well with bitter coffee.

Castella (Japanese pound cake)

The egg and honey in castella pairs well with latte's milk, making it taste like custard cream.

Buttered toast

Richness in butter pairs well with bitter coffee.

Red bean bun

Just like how red bean bun goes well with milk, Japanese sweets and latte is a great match.

SPECIAL SUPPORT

MARUKA CORPORATION
http://www.maruka-grp.co.jp

De'Longhi Japan
http://www.delonghi.co.jp

Katashimo Winery
http://www.kashiwara-wine.com

HARIO CO., LTD.
http://www.hario.com

Nespresso Club
http://www.nespresso.com

Nestle Japan
http://nestle.jp/faq/index.php

Takanashi Milk Products Co., Ltd.
http://www.takanashi-milk.co.jp

Coca-Cola (Japan) Company, Limited
http://cocacola.co.jp

CALPIS Co., Ltd.
http://www.calpis.co.jp

TOEI KOGYO CO., LTD
http://www.toei-inc.co.jp

Kikkoman Corporation
http://www.kikkoman.co.jp

STREAMER COFFEE COMPANY
http://www.streamercoffee.com

Hiroshi Sawada

Originally from the Osaka Prefecture, Hiroshi Sawada is a world-renowned barista and latte artist. Upon graduating from Kinki University School of Commerce and Education, Sawada joined the team at Kinokuniya International Supermarket. In 2008 he became the first Asian to win the Latte Art World Championship in Seattle, WA. In 2010, he went on to open his first independent coffee shop, Streamer Coffee Company, in the center of Shibuya, Tokyo. Since then, he has opened nearly two dozen Streamer Coffee Company locations across Japan, as well as Sawada Coffee in Chicago, IL in 2015.

HIROSHI SAWADA'S
THE BARISTA BOOK

First Skyhorse Publishing Edition 2018

Skyhorse Publishing books may be purchased in bulk at special discounts for sales promotion, corporate gifts, fund-raising, or educational purposes. Special editions can also be created to specifications. For details, contact the Special Sales Department, Skyhorse Publishing, 307 West 36th Street, 11th Floor, New York, NY 10018 or info@skyhorsepublishing.com.

Skyhorse® and Skyhorse Publishing® are registered trademarks of Skyhorse Publishing, Inc.®, a Delaware corporation.

Visit our website at www.skyhorsepublishing.com.

10 9 8 7

Library of Congress Cataloging-in-Publication Data is available on file.

Cover design by Michael Short
Cover photograph: Transworld Japan Inc.
Interior artwork: Transworld Japan Inc.
Interior photography: Transworld Japan Inc.

ISBN: 978-1-63158-218-9

Printed in the United States of America